Sweet Dreams
for Little Ones

Sweet Dreams
for Little Ones

by Michael G. Pappas

HarperSanFrancisco

A Division of HarperCollins*Publishers*

The Values Goals are adapted for use in this book with permission of Thomas C. Wright, Inc.

Illustrations by Else Wenz-Vietor are taken from the children's book *Guten Abend, Gute Nacht*, published in 1927 by Stalling Verlag GmbH, Oldenburg, Federal Republic of Germany. Used by permission of the publisher.

Book design: Holly Ramsey

Library of Congress Catalog Card Number: 81-69553
ISBN: 0-86683-641-1

Printed in the United States of America

91 92 93 VIK 14 13 12 11 10 9

To Julian and Brendan, whose loving enthusiasm helped in the development and use of this material

Table of Contents

Introduction	9
Getting Ready	10
Gently Growing	15
Baby You	16
Big Hug	18
New Friend	20
Getting Bigger	22
Gifts from the Planet	25
Beach Bubble	26
Sleigh Ride	28
Cabin Snow	31
Sailboat to Toy Island	34
Touching Life	37
Tree You	38
Plant Love	40
Hurt Bird	42

Helping   45

Monster Scare   46
Kid Strong   48
Rescue   51
Lost Child   53
Great Giver   55

Onward and Upward   59

For the Children   60
Made of Light   62

Values Goals   64

Introduction

Sweet Dreams for Little Ones is more than a children's story book. It is an exciting and innovative approach to storytelling unlike any you have ever known. This is a book designed to open doors in your child's mind, to stimulate imagination, and to develop in your child the ability to accept and nurture positive creative fantasy, an essential ingredient for success in childhood and adult life. We hope this book of tales will help your child grow closer to you and experience both greater relaxation and concentration while being entertained by these stories. This novel storytelling process takes into account your busy schedule and requires only a ten minute nightly or weekly investment.

The eighteen stories in *Sweet Dreams for Little Ones* are fantasy vignettes which focus on one or more of the basic needs known to affect all human behavior: affection, enlightenment, respect, responsibility, power, skill, wealth, and well-being.* The vignette themes range from family love to adventure on the high seas, from enjoying the beauty of life to exploring its mysteries, from watching the froth of swelling surf to being strong enough to help others in need.

These rich tales use guided imagery or verbal cues to help your child see herself or himself as the story's central character, the important person around whom all the action evolves. The most unique and powerful part of using this guided imagery is that your child does more than listen to a story in which someone else is acting. Instead your little one sees herself or himself on center stage with all the excitement unfolding in an engaging scenario. What fun then to go to sleep at night! What a delight for little ones to enjoy Sweet Dreams!

*These needs are known as Value Goals and are described on page 64.

Getting Ready

Relaxation and concentration are important for your child if she or he is to enjoy *Sweet Dreams for Little Ones* and enter into the stories. For this reason, you may want to help your child relax before you begin to read. Although the following steps are not absolutely necessary in experiencing each story, we do highly recommend them:

1. Take care of your child's nighttime rituals before reading. This includes getting a drink, going to the bathroom, and discussing any worrisome problems. This is important for both you and your little one, for it helps make sure that your story time will be free of interruptions.

2. Do some warm-ups to help settle your child's mind and body. (See pages 11-12.)

3. Encourage your child to stay in the relaxation pose during the story (See page 13.) Before reading, invite your little one to listen to your words and try to see the changing pictures of the story in his or her mind.

4. Read slowly enough to give your child time to form the mental picture yet quickly enough to keep her or his mind from wandering between sentences.

5. End each story by saying ''Sweet dreams'' and giving your child a hug and a kiss good-night. Or ask a few questions about your little one's response to the reading. This may help your child pull together the experience he or she has just had as well as provide you with some valuable insights. However, save any extensive questioning for the next morning.

After the reading you want your child's mind to remain peaceful so that she or he will enjoy sweet dreams.

Warm-ups

To help your little one relax and settle his or her body and mind, you may want to have him or her do the following two exercises. Before telling or reading the first vignette, explain the first exercise to your child, then massage your little one's body or demonstrate how to massage.

1. Deep Breathing

This exercise will relax and purify your child's body. (Most people inhale too little oxygen during the course of the day, using the lungs to only one-third their capacity. Over time this inadequate supply of oxygen speeds up the aging process, impairs organ function, and has a generally unhealthy effect on the body.) Deep breathing will increase your little one's well-being.

Procedure: As your child is sitting upright in bed, explain the reasons for the deep breathing exercises. Then give the following instructions: ''Close your eyes. (Pause.) Breathe in slowly and deeply while I count to four. (Count.) Now hold your breath while I count to four again. (Count.) Now I want you to breathe out slowly and deeply and I'll count to four another time. (Count.) Now let's do this again.'' Your child may soon want to do his or her own mental counting for this exercise. Then sit quietly on the bed while your little one does the deep breathing exercise twice.

2. Massage

The purpose of a three-minute massage before storytelling is twofold: to affirm your love for your child and to create a wholesome effect on his or her body. Massage stimulates the entire nervous system, relaxes the muscles, and enhances blood circulation, thus promoting better health. We end the massage at the feet because nerves from the entire body are here. Massaging the soles of the feet centers the entire body.

Procedure: Massage your child's scalp deliberately with the fingers of both your hands. From the scalp, move to the face, massaging it firmly, keeping one hand on each side of it. Include the ears and neck, then move to the shoulders. Next, massage your child's back, chest and buttocks. Then place both hands around one of your child's arms and begin massaging down to the hand. Massage the hand, giving special attention to each finger. Repeat the process with the other arm and hand. Next, place your hands around one leg and massage it down to the ankle. Repeat the process with the other leg. Then bring both hands to one foot and vigorously massage the underside and toes. From one foot move to the other. When you conclude, hold your child's foot until your energy dissipates (you will feel this happening). After a few evenings in which you massage your child's body, he or she may want to practice this massage while you sit quietly and watch.

The Relaxation Pose

The relaxation pose will help your child to attain a quieting of both mind and body. We recommend this posture because of its comfortable and balanced design and because it will help your child block out distractions and enhance her or his concentration. Following the massage and immediately before you begin to read, encourage your child to assume the relaxation pose.

Procedure: Say to your little one, "I want you to lie flat on your back now with your legs straight out on the bed and your feet relaxed. Point your toes upward toward the ceiling. Now put your arms down by your side. Relax your body. Now turn your hands so that your palms face the ceiling. Close your eyes and let your body remain very quiet and at peace. I want you to stay just like this, relaxed and at peace, as I read this story to you."

Gently Growing

Baby You

Imagine yourself as a tiny baby just a few months old lying in your bed. . . .Your eyes are closed. . . .Feel the blanket as your tiny legs kick at it. Feel your feet as they touch the blanket. . . .Your little arms are bent, and your hands are tightly closed. . . .Your mouth is half open, and your tongue is resting in your mouth, which has no teeth.

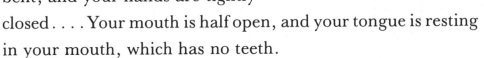

See your eyes open slowly. . . .Look at the ceiling of your room. You notice the sun's light shining through the window. . . .Look at the tiny pieces of dust as they pass through the sunlight and float in the air. Look around the room. . .and see the different things that this baby you likes to look at. . . .Now look very closely at your favorite things in the room. . . .

Listen. . . .In another room you can hear someone saying very nice things about you. . . .Listen to the things that person is saying....Now some other people are talking and walking toward you....Watch carefully as they come to your bed and each one kisses you on the forehead. Look at the smiles on their faces as they bend over....Listen carefully as each person says, "_____(child's name), I love you, and you are really someone very special."...Listen to everyone say this....

When these people have finished telling you how wonderful you are, look over toward the door, and you will see yourself standing near it....The real today you is standing there looking at baby you....Now, today you is walking toward the bed....Today you gives baby you a big hug....Today you says to baby you, "I love you, too, _____(child's name), and you are really someone precious. But just wait until you get to be as old as I am! You will be an even more beautiful person then...."

Now watch as baby you smiles a big smile...and disappears inside of today you....As that happens you feel so much love....Just feel all the love inside of you now as you think about baby you....*Sweet Dreams!*

Big Hug

Think of someone you would really like a big hug from. Maybe this person is someone you live with . . . or maybe someone you haven't seen in a while . . . . Think about what the person looks like who is standing facing you . . . . See the face smiling and the eyes looking at you . . . . Feel the softness of the eyes loving you . . . .

Slowly reach out and touch that person's cheeks by gently moving your fingertips along them . . . . Feel the little tingle in your fingertips . . . .

Now slowly lower your arms to your side and say, . . . "I would really like a big hug right now." . . . As you say this, watch the person's arms open wide for you . . . . Listen as he or she says "I would like a big hug from you right now . . . ."

Open your arms and hug each other tightly and stay

still....While you are hugging, imagine that the two of you are melting together so that you are really just one person....Being this close feels good!...You never want to break away....Hear yourselves breathing together....Feel your hearts beating....Feel that you are actually floating a little bit off the ground....Stay floating for a few moments...then lower yourselves back to the soft ground beneath your feet....

Now say, "Thank you for sharing love." Let your arms drop back to your side and step back from the person....Look at him or her once again, noticing the face and eyes, and say..."Good-bye." Then walk off until you are far away....

Getting a big hug from someone you love feels so good. And now you know one thing for sure....If ever you miss this person, just remember that you can bring him or her back again any time you like....*Sweet Dreams!*

New Friend

Think of someone you really want to get to know better. You want this person to like you a lot. . . . Maybe this is someone you don't know too well right now or someone you are just beginning to become friends with. . . .

See the person's face smiling and looking at you. Notice his or her eyes. . . . Now think of something that you would like the person to see you do. . . . You could do something that would help explain what kind of child you are. . . .

Appear at the place where you will do that special something. . . . Now begin. . . and keep doing it. . . . Look at what you are doing and watch your new friend's face as you show him or her something that is really important. When you finish, walk away. . . .

Now you would like to let your new friend meet an old friend of yours or someone you already love very much. . . . Walk over to your old friend. . . . Your old, or your "already" friend likes your new friend, and your new friend likes your already friend. . . . Watch them talking to each other about what a great person you are. . . .

You want to do one more thing for your new friend. You want to show your friend something of yours that you are really proud of. . . . Walk over to the place where you keep this special thing and place your hands on it. . . . Tell your new friend all about it, what you like about it, and what you like to do with it. . . . Let your new friend do something with it and listen as your new friend tells you what a really nice thing it is. . . .

Now, before your new friend leaves, you want to go to one more place. . . . The two of you are going to the place where you like to spend a lot of time. . . . Show off your special place. . . . Now listen as your new friend tells you what a kind and fun person you are and what good friends the two of you will be. . . . Put your arms around each other for a nice little hug, and say good-bye for today and hello for forever. . . .

As your new friend leaves, you think of what a good time you've had together and of some more things you would like to show him or her the next time you meet. . . . *Sweet Dreams!*

Getting Bigger

Sometimes you need to get big to understand just what things look like from far away. . . . Now first, you must go out into an open field with lots of space. . . . Stand there looking down at the ground and carefully look at what you see. . . .

Now look around and find a tree. . . . Over there is a tree, a big beautiful leaf-covered tree. . . . You want to look at the top of the tree, so you must use some special magic. . . . Reach up to the sky and push up with your hands. . . . Push hard. . . . Keep pushing, and watch as you keep getting bigger and bigger until your head is above the tree. . . . Now see what you can see on the top of the tree. . . .

Walk away from the tree and look up at the clouds in the sky. . . . Seeing those clouds right in front of you would be nice. . . . Well, all you have to do is stretch your arms up to the sky, and you'll keep getting bigger and bigger until your head is in the clouds. . . . See how foggy the sky looks up in the clouds. . . . This is great fun, but you want to get even bigger.

So once again reach your arms up to the sky and push up with your hands until you begin to stretch again. . . . You stretch and

stretch until you get so big that you begin to float up from the earth into the sky like a big floating giant. If you look down at the earth now you can see its round shape, but it still looks very, very big....So you must become bigger still....So stretch once again....and now when you look at the earth it's like a ball....Look at the ocean and look at the land....Look at all the other balls spinning around the gigantic, bright, hot sun....
Float over and feel the sun's heat....Look at all the beautiful colors of the planets....Look at all the stars....

   If you stretch again...you become so big that suddenly everything looks small and close. You are completely surrounded by thousands of little suns and planets and stars....Space is so crowded by them now that as you float along you keep bumping into them....You are so big now that you wonder what would happen if you grew bigger and bigger....

   Well, let's try again....Reach up with your arms and stretch. And my goodness,...you are so big now that everything in the whole universe seems small and crowded. You can hardly see past the planets and suns and stars....They are so close that you can feel them every time you move....

You wonder what will happen if you get bigger one more time. . . . You decide to find out. . . . So you stretch up your arms and see that the sky is so crowded now that you can't even see anything. Everything is pressing against you so closely that you almost have to swim through space to get anywhere. . . . Feel yourself swimming through space. . . .

You see a light, so you try to swim toward it. You get closer and closer, and all of a sudden you are back on earth. . . . You are swimming in the ocean and you can see several people on shore waving to you. . . . Everyone you love is standing there smiling and waving for you to swim to shore. . . . You are happy to be back, and as you swim to shore you think about your wonderful, long trip floating through space and what it was like to get bigger and bigger. . . . *Sweet Dreams!* ☆ ☆

Gifts from the Planet

Beach Bubble

You are walking along an ocean beach....Your feet are cool on the wet sand....The warm waves are crashing at your feet....As the waves push in and fall back out along the beach...foam and bubbles are made....With the warm, blowing wind slide the foam and bubbles along the beach....Look at the waves moving along the beach....

Suddenly the wind stops and the foam and bubbles remain still....Look carefully at one of the tiny bubbles....Notice the sunlight painting it many beautiful colors. The bubble is slowly getting bigger and bigger....Now it's as big as you are....This must be some kind of magic....

As you look around the beach you see that many of the bubbles surrounding you are also getting bigger until all that you can see around you are big and little bubbles floating in the air....Look at all the colors....The bubbles are all still now....Not one of them is moving....

Walk slowly through the bubbles on the beach and stop and look into one....You can clearly see inside it a beautiful flower garden with flowers that are white and yellow and red and blue.

26

...These flowers are growing inside the bubble. ...Smell the flowers....You can hardly believe your eyes and your nose....

Walk around the beach to see what else you can find in these magical bubbles....Another one is floating a few steps away....Walk up to it.... Inside it you can see several people looking up at you and reaching out to give you a hug. ...Smile. ...Look at their faces....You know them....

Walk on and you will see another bubble....If you look into it you will see children playing together....They are happy and are having fun....Look carefully to see what they are doing....

Look at this next bubble. In it you see a child in a bed asleep. Someone is coming into the room and pulling warm covers over this child....

As you stand on the beach looking at all these beautiful bubbles floating in the air, you decide to look at just one more.... So you walk up to another bubble and look into it. You see someone who looks just like you standing on a bubble-covered beach, and the child is looking into one of the many bubbles....

Sweet Dreams!

Sleigh Ride

You are standing inside a big, red, wooden barn....The cold winter wind is blowing snow outside....You are dressed warmly and are getting ready to do something special.... This barn is out in the country. In this quiet place you will find farms and fields and dirt roads, but not many people. The houses are far apart....

As you stand in the barn, you see a sleigh with two white horses waiting to pull it....The sleigh is black with front and back seats....The seats are red and black and made of soft leather.... The front seat is for you, because you will be the driver....The back seat is for anyone you want to bring along on the ride....

Walk over to the sleigh and climb into the front seat. Sit down....This is a good time for everyone else to get into the sleigh....Turn around and look at the faces of the people riding in the sleigh with you....

The horses are magical, and they will listen to you and do anything you tell them to do....Tell them to walk slowly....Feel the sleigh starting to move forward through the snow....Now tell the horses to go a little faster....Feel the motion as the sleigh goes faster through the snow, and look at the tracks the sleigh and the horses are making. . . .

Listen as the people in the back seat are laughing and having a good time. . . .Turn around and look at them . . . their red cheeks and noses . . . and at the snow that is blowing onto their hair and eyebrows. . . . Stick out your tongue and taste the cold snowflakes that drop onto it. . . . Look over at all the trees . . . at their branches . . . which are full of snow. . . . Smell the clean, cold air. . . . Feel the sleigh moving forward. . . . Now as you look ahead you can see a rabbit running through the snow and calling your name. . . . "Hi, _____ (child's name)!"

Up ahead on the road you see a reindeer standing and looking lost. . . . Tell the horses to slow down. . . . and stop. . . . The reindeer asks, "Do you know where the North Pole is? I'm supposed to meet someone there.". . . One of the people in the back seat says with finger pointed, "I know where it is. The North Pole is that-a-way.". . . The reindeer says, "Thank you so much. . . . I've got to go now because I will be late for something if I don't get back."

Almost like magic the reindeer flies up into the snowy sky until you can't see it anymore. . . . Someone says, ''I wonder where that reindeer is going.''. . . Tell the horses to start walking again. . . . As the sleigh continues along, you think about the wonderful time you are having. . . . And you wonder what other fun things will happen on this special sleigh ride. . . . *Sweet Dreams!*

Cabin Snow

You are a child long ago during the days of log cabins and no electricity. Horses were used instead of cars, and everything was old-fashioned....

You are lying in your bed....You open your eyes and look around at your room in the log cabin. You have candles for light, and you can see the walls and ceiling. Everything in the room is made by hand....

Look at the wooden dresser....It has a burning candle on it. Watch the candle glowing yellow....The room is quiet. Grown-ups are sitting in the main room, which is like a living room and kitchen....Your home is heated by the fireplace. This a cold winter night, so the fire will have to be kept burning all evening....

You feel rather cold, so you get out of your bed, put shoes on your feet, and walk into the main room. The grown-ups in the room are asleep in the chairs. You walk over to the fireplace and hold out your hands to be warmed by the fire....You carefully place logs in the fire....As you do, you notice the little sparks that go flying up into the chimney....

31

A pot with a hot drink for you is hanging on a hook by the fire. The glowing fire is keeping your drink warm....You slowly remove the pot from the hook and pour yourself some in a cup. As you raise the cup to your mouth, you can smell and taste the delicious hot drink. Feel how warm the cup is in your hands....

Now walk over to the window and pull the curtains to the side....The window is coated with ice, so breathe a warm spot onto it....Now you can see through it. Look into the cold winter night at the snow falling from the sky....Look at the snow covering everything it touches....Listen to the wind blowing the snow through the air....

You finish your drink and close the curtains....Now walk over and softly kiss the sleeping grown-ups....Walk back into your room and get an extra blanket from the foot of your bed. Spread it over the bed....Now take off your shoes while you blow out the candle and crawl into bed....

The bed is so cold that you have to move your arms and legs back and forth very fast against the sheets to make the bed warm. . . . Pull the covers up so they feel comfortable. Listen to the snow blowing outside. . . . How good being inside under the covers feels. . . . You lie there and wonder what everything will look like in the morning. . . . *Sweet Dreams!*

Sailboat to Toy Island

You are sailing to an island in the middle of the ocean.... The sun is bright.... The rolling ocean is blue, and the waves keep splashing against the sides of the boat, throwing a fine spray of water into the sunlight.... The warm wind is blowing and filling the sails with gentle energy....

You are standing at the wheel of the boat, and other kids you've invited along are with you.... Feel the wind blowing the salty spray onto your face... and smell it as you breathe in.... Feel the wind blowing your hair and eyebrows.... Now look up at the sky.... It is blue with only a few wispy white clouds in it....

You see a few seagulls in the sky, so you know that you are coming closer to Toy Island.... As you hear the seagulls flapping in the air and the ocean splashing against the boat, you start to think about what Toy Island will be like.

On this island you will find every kind of toy in the world. On this island kids from all over the world show other kids how to use these toys.... Everyone has fun sharing and taking care of toys.... You will be staying on Toy Island for a few days, and all the kids on the boat are excited....What fun you will have when you get there....Imagine all the great toys and games you will play with....Think of all the kids you will play with....There will probably be some toys that will be fun to play with alone....

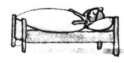

Now if you look straight ahead, you will see the island. Grip the boat's wheel and steer the boat toward the island.... As you are standing there at the wheel you stop and think that you are making many people happy by bringing them to Toy Island.... And this stay at Toy Island promises to be a fun time for you too!...*Sweet Dreams!* ☆

Touching Life

Tree You

Becoming invisible would really be fun. You could walk inside of something and know just how being that thing would feel....Let's try walking inside a tree....Find a big old tree with long branches and covered with leaves....Walk up to it....

Now, because you are invisible, walk right through this tree and stop when you get inside....You are now standing inside the tree, but you can see through it to the outside....Hold your hands up into the tree and make your arms stretch up...up...until they stretch right into the branches....You are in the tree with your arms in the branches....

Now stretch your hands and fingers so that they will fit into the smaller branches....Now each arm is inside a branch and every finger is inside a smaller branch....Now move your arms and fingers slowly and feel the branches moving back and forth.... Listen to the leaves on your fingers as you move them about in the air....

Stretch your legs downward into the roots of the tree. Feel your feet and toes fit into the smaller roots as they too stretch downward....You can't move the roots because the earth is packed tightly around them. . . . Feel the food and water energy traveling up through your roots . . . up your trunk into your branches, and out of your leaves. . . . Imagine a tiny river of energy flowing from your roots slowly up . . . and up . . . and finally out into the air. . . . This energy is the air that animals need to breathe. . . .

It is summertime now. . . . Feel the hot sun shining down on your leaf-covered branches. . . . Now feel the rain washing all that summer dust off of you and cooling you. . . .

Autumn comes, and your leaves dry up and fall to the ground. . . . You begin to feel sleepy and prepare to rest for the winter. . . . While asleep in the winter, you feel the icy winds blow snow at you . . . sometimes piling it up around you. . . . But then you awaken with spring as the birds tickle you with their busy nest building. . . .

Now you are wide awake. . . . Step out of the tree and leave it behind you. . . . Look at it once again. . . . Being a tree was really special. . . . Trees are very special. . . . Imagine what other kinds of things somebody could become. . . . *Sweet Dreams!*

Plant Love

If plants could talk they would probably ask us to do many things to help them....You can do something to help plants....You will need two things to do the job....The first thing you will need is a spoon....Find an old one somewhere and put it into your pocket or hold onto it....It will be used for digging up the earth around the plants....

The second thing you will need to help plants is a water pitcher or something with which you can water the plants....Hold the container in your hand and walk over to the sink or to a place where you can get some water....Hold the container under the faucet, and with the other hand turn on the water....While the pitcher is filling, notice the bubbles forming under the fast running water....Turn off the water when the pitcher is full, and remove it. You are now ready to help the plants....

Walk to a place where you know many plants grow....If you look around you will see a flower that is looking very dry and leaning over as if it is ready to die....Listen carefully as it asks you, ''Please dig up my earth and give me some water!'' You are surprised to hear a flower talking, but you begin working right

away. . . .

First dig up the earth using the spoon like a shovel. . . . While you are digging, you are careful to keep the spoon away from the flower's stem. . . . When you finish, give the flower some water from the pitcher. . . . Listen to how the flower says "Thank you!". . . Say something good back to it. . . . Watch the flower straighten up and look beautiful because you gave it your love and care. . . .

Now you hear something else asking for help. . . . Look around and listen carefully. . . . As you listen, you hear tiny voices crying out together. . . . You look over to a tree branch that has fallen on some tiny blades of grass. . . . The branch is blocking out the sunlight. If you do not remove it, the grass will die. . . .

Walk over, pick up the branch, and toss it out of the way. . . . Listen to the tiny voices of the blades of grass thanking you for saving their lives. . . . Give them a little water and see how happy their faces are as the sunlight starts warming them. . . . As you finish with the grass, think how much help plants really do need. . . .

And you really did make them happy by helping them stay alive. . . . But that is just the kind of person you are. . . . *Sweet Dreams!*

Hurt Bird

You are sitting outside in the summertime. . . . Feel and smell the soft cool grass beneath you. . . . The sun is warm on your skin, and a light breeze is blowing. . . .

You sit there running your hands over the grass. . . . Then a hurt bird comes fluttering along and drops to the ground in front of you. . . . It has a few drops of blood on it. . . . It is breathing and can move around. . . . Stand up on the grass. Look at the bird . . . and slowly walk closer to it. The hurt bird is becoming a little scared and is flopping around. . . .

Gently put your hands on its soft, white feathers and pick it up. . . . It relaxes a little when it knows you want to help. Hold the bird carefully as you walk home with it. Say something to the bird to help it feel better. . . .

When you get home you find a large cardboard box. . . . Carefully place the bird into the open box. . . . Now find someone to help you. . . . Explain that you will need some food and water for the bird. . . .

Sit and watch and hope that the bird will get better. . . . Ask the bird to get well. . . . Now the food and water are brought. Put them into the box and watch the bird eat some food and drink some water. . . .

Now watch it rest. . . . Stand up and walk away from the box for a while . . . . hoping that the bird will get better and knowing that you have done much to help a dying animal live. . . . And think how lucky that bird is to have someone as caring as you come along. . . . *Sweet Dreams!*

Helping

Monster Scare

See yourself on a picnic with your friends. . . . No grown-ups are along. . . . Everybody is having a good time playing in the grass, feeling the cool breeze and the warmth of the sun.

A dark forest is next to the picnic place. . . . Look at the forest. See the tall trees. . . . See how dark the forest is inside. Listen now and you can hear a terrible roaring noise coming from within the forest. . . . And suddenly a gigantic green and black and red and yellow monster steps out of the dark forest. It is looking at you and it is very scary. . . .

Look at the monster's face . . . and hands . . . and eyes . . . and nose . . . and feet. . . . This monster is having a good time making all the children afraid. . . . You are going to have to do something to stop all this scaring. . . . Suddenly you remember that someone has brought pepper along on the picnic. . . . You empty the pepper shaker into your hand . . . and close your hand tightly. . . .

Now the monster is acting even worse, and everyone is really afraid. . . . With the pepper in your hand, sneak up to the monster. . . . As soon as you get next to it, throw the pepper right into its face. Watch as the monster suddenly backs away and begins to sneeze and sneeze and rub its eyes...and sneeze some more....Now it is acting very embarrassed and starts getting smaller and smaller....Watch as it becomes smaller. It begins to look less scary. When you see that the monster is not going to scare the children anymore, hand it a wet towel to wipe its eyes...and give it some tissue to blow the pepper from its nose....

Now look the monster in the eyes and say,..."Kids are for loving...not for scaring....And if you want to stay around here, you will have to be nice to everyone."...Look at the monster and notice that it is slightly afraid of you....But instead of scaring it, hold its hand and say,..."Come on, you can play with us. I think we can all be friends. You would really be a lot of fun to play with."...

Once this monster used to think that scaring children was the only way to get attention....And you are the first person to ever care about it....As you are playing and watching the monster get along happily with your friends...you begin to think how afraid the monster must have been to believe that it always had to scare everyone....And you feel good because you have helped someone to be happy and to learn more about children....*Sweet Dreams!*

Kid Strong

Your name is _____ (child's name) Strong. You have special powers.... You are very strong and can lift anything that you want to no matter how big or heavy it is.... You use your power only to help people....

One day as you are walking along a sidewalk, you see something terrible happen.... A big truck has turned over, and the driver is inside the truck. But he is not hurt too badly.... See that the truck is upside down ... and see the front of the truck and the driver inside of it.... Hear the driver shouting for help....

Run to the truck.... Carefully place your hands on it and begin to lift it up.... Now feel your arms pulling up the truck.... Feel the truck's weight and keep lifting slowly...slowly. See the truck turning over until it is right side up.... You are doing all this.... Now the truck is standing up straight....

The driver shouts to you that he has a way of getting out now.... Look and see the driver climbing out the window and walking over to you.... See the driver's face looking at you ... and listen as you hear him say, "Thank you, I don't know what I would have done without you."...Say something nice back to the driver....

The next day you are walking along, going somewhere to play. You see a large tree limb that has broken during a storm and crashed down over someone's house. Nobody has been hurt, but the tree has put a big hole in the roof of the house....

Look up and see the gigantic limb....As you walk closer to the house, you see the people who live in it. They are outside looking up at the roof. You hear them say, "We can't fix the roof because the tree is in the way, and if we cut part of it, it will roll down and cause more damage."...Ask them if they need your help...and listen as they say, "Yes, thank you. We bet you are someone who can really help us....We'll hold the ladder for you and watch you as you climb up to the roof."

You feel glad that there is a grown-up to help you, because climbing on the roof might be dangerous....Now climb up the ladder carefully until you get to the top. Pull yourself up and carefully stand on the rooftop. Look below for a place on the ground where nobody is standing so you can safely throw down the tree limb....Now place your hands on the trunk and give the tree a big lift. . . . Keep holding and lifting. Then push that limb up over your head and give it a big shove. See the tree limb falling into an open part of the yard. Listen to it as it crashes below. . . .

Now carefully climb down from the roof and listen as everyone thanks you for your great help. . . . You say, ''Thanks for letting me help.'' You walk away from the house and back to where you were going before you stopped here. . . .

As you walk away, you wonder in what other ways you, _____(child's name) Strong, might be able to help others. . . . *Sweet Dreams!*

Rescue

Think of someone you really like and whom you would like to rescue from danger. See a picture in your mind of this person.... See him or her smiling and looking at you.... Now imagine that you are standing on the side of a swimming pool while the person you really like is swimming. Nobody else is around....

You are walking along the side of the pool.... Feel the hard cement beneath your feet.... Look at the water move in little waves shining in the sun.... Suddenly you hear splashing and calling for help from the person in the pool. Look and see the person trying to keep from going under....

You must help fast.... Look around the pool side for a long rescue pole.... You see one on the other side of the pool.... Run around and pick it up.... Hold it out over the water and let the drowning person grab it.... Feel the pull from the person you are saving. Now pull him or her to the edge of the pool.... Feel your hands holding the pole tightly and your legs working hard to keep you pulling....

When you get the person to the edge of the pool... see that he or she is able to climb out of the water onto the pool side. A towel is

51

on the chair next to the pool....Grab it and help dry your friend....Now look at the face of this lucky person....A smile of love is on this person's face, and it is just for you....Listen to the way he or she says "Thank you"...and feel the big wet hug you are getting....Give a good hug back....Then think how much you are appreciated and how lucky you were to be able to save someone's life as you did....*Sweet Dreams!*

Lost Child

Imagine that you are walking near your home
and you see a child sitting on the side of the road
crying and looking down at the ground. . . . As
you walk up to the child, you say, "Hey, what's
wrong?" He answers, "I'm very sad and lonely."
Hold out your hand and firmly take hold of his
hand. Pull him up so that both of you are
standing. . . .

Place your hand on the child's back and rub it gently as you
say, "Come on over to our home. We'll help you." Walk with him
back to your home, and when you get inside . . . ask his name . . .
and telephone for help. . . .

Now go into the kitchen and ask your guest to sit down on a
chair at the table. . . . Walk over to the refrigerator and open it. . . .
Look around until you see something for the two of you to eat and
drink. . . . If the food needs to be prepared, then take care of
that. . . . Now put a plate of food on the table and ask him to eat
something. If you are hungry, have some food too. . . . But make
sure that your guest gets enough to eat. . . .

Next walk over and pour something to drink into a glass and carry it over to the table. . . . Listen as your guest thanks you. . . . Walk over and give him a pat on the back and say, "Everything will be all right." You can see a great big smile on his face. . . . You smile back. . . .

You hear a knock at the door. . . . You walk over to the door, but before you have a chance to find out who's there, the child happily shouts out, "Hey, I know who that is!" and runs over to open the door. . . . In the door stands the person the child had lost! They hug each other and say a few words . . . and turn to you and thank you for the very kind thing you did. . . . You smile . . . give your new friend a hug . . . and say how much fun playing together might be some time. . . . As they leave, you think how lucky you were to be able to help a lost child like that. . . . *Sweet Dreams!*

Great Giver

You are the Great Giver...a special kind of person...a magical kind of person....

Since you were just a little baby, you've been giving to others. But you have a special magic....Your magic is that as long as somebody needs something, you will have something to give.

Look, you have your own horse....On its back is a big leather saddle with a large saddle bag on each side....Walk up to the horse. Its color is black with big spots of white....Touch the horse's warm nose gently and pet its head. See the horse's eyes....Now walk around the left side of the horse and place your left foot in the stirrup that is hanging from the saddle....Grab the saddle horn with both hands and pull yourself up onto the saddle....Swing your right leg over the saddle and place your right foot in the right stirrup....Now pick up the reins and command the horse to walk by saying, "Walk."...

As your horse walks along, you notice how far up from the ground you are. Look at the ground beneath you as your horse's hooves pass over it....As you ride on, you notice a child walking to school .... She wears very old and torn shoes which do not

cover her feet. . . . Tell the horse to stop by saying, "Stop." . . .
Call out to the child, "Excuse me. . . . I am the Great Giver. . . .
May I give you a new pair of shoes?". . .

Watch the smile on the girl's face as she says yes to
you. . . . Reach into the saddlebag and pull out a pair of
shoes and hand them to the girl. . . . Listen as she thanks
you. . . . Say to her, "I like to give to others. Thank you
for letting me give to you."

As the girl is putting on her shoes, pick up your horse's reins
again and command your horse to walk by saying, "Walk." As
you ride along the road you look ahead and notice that you are
riding straight toward a playground. You can see several children
playing. . . . One child is crying. Some of the others have been
mean to him. Pull back on the reins and tell your horse to stop by
saying, "Stop." Your horse stops right in front of the sad child.
"You look very sad and hurt. . . . I am the Great Giver. . . . I like to
give. . . . May I please give you a ride on my horse?" Still sad, the
boy says yes. . . . Hold your left hand down to him and pull him up
onto the horse behind you. . . . Once he is on the horse, turn around
and look at him. . . . See that he is smiling now and looks very

happy. . . . Pick up the reins again and tell your horse to walk by saying, "Walk.". . . As you and he ride along on your horse, the boy spots some other friends who are waving at him and calling to him. He gets excited and asks you if he can get down now. . . . Stop the horse by pulling back on the reins and saying "Stop." Watch as the boy jumps off and goes running happily to play with his friends. . . . He turns around and shouts "Thanks!" to you. You shout back, "You're welcome!" Pick up the reins again and command your horse to walk by saying, "Walk." As the horse walks on you look around and wonder what other ways you, the Great Giver, can give. . . . *Sweet Dreams!* ☆

Onward and Upward

For the Children

Imagine a time when things are really sad on earth. Dark clouds hide the sun, and the people on earth have no light to see with. Because of their special power at this time, only the children can help....

Walk outside into the darkness and hear the sounds of other children singing everywhere....Walk closer to the sound, and in the darkness, you can see children in a long line that seems to stretch forever....Become part of that line by standing between two children and holding hands with them....

All the children are holding hands and singing...but nobody is really playing because everybody knows that a very important job must be done....

The magic will begin when the children squeeze each other's hands. So squeeze the hands on each side of you....Suddenly you all become glowing with beautiful bluish-white light all over your bodies....Look at the other children glowing like you. Feel the love from the light....

Squeeze the children's hands again....The whole line quietly begins to float with you up into the air...still glowing beautifully. . . . Look at the children on each side of you floating in the air. . . .

Squeeze hands again. . . . Now the line of children starts moving slowly like a big train. . . . The line makes a circle all the way around the world. . . . Feel yourself moving slowly around the world. . . .

Squeeze hand agains, and the line begins circling the earth faster than a jet plane. . . . The line of children looks like a blue-white ring of light around the world, and this ring is melting the clouds. . . . The whole beautiful earth is glowing. . . . The darkness is gone. . . .

Now squeeze the children's hands once more, and the movement stops. . . . All the children float slowly back down to earth. . . . You are still holding hands and still glowing light. . . .

All the children are going back to their homes taking light to everyone. . . . Now the dark clouds will stay away from the planet . . . and the light will shine . . . as long as there are children like you. . . . *Sweet Dreams!*

Made of Light

You are the pilot of a star ship. It is cruising along in outer space....You have just switched the controls to automatic, which means that the ship will pilot itself and you won't have to sit at the controls....

You are out of your seat and floating inside the star ship. Look at all the buttons and switches on the cabin wall....Look at all the different colored lights on the wall....

You are now resting by lying flat and floating in the air inside your ship....Feel yourself on your back peacefully floating....As you lie flat you see a tiny white light coming toward you from space .... It comes closer and closer until it touches the ship, and almost like magic the ship disappears....

And there you are floating in space....You are not afraid because you know the light and have seen it somewhere before. You remember that it is a friend of some kind....

The tiny ball of white light touches your foot, and as you lie in space your leg disappears all the way up to the knee....Then the rest of your leg disappears....The tiny white light then moves to your other foot and that leg disappears up to the knee....Then the rest of your leg disappears. You are now floating in space with no legs. . . . You feel funny, but you are not worried. . . . You feel lighter than before.

The tiny ball of white light now moves to your hand and it disappears. . . . Then the light goes up the arm to the elbow and that part of your arm disappears. . . . Then the light moves up to the shoulder and your upper arm disappears. . . . Now your one arm and both your legs have disappeared, so the light moves to the hand of your other arm. . . . It, too, disappears. . . . Then the light moves again . . . and the whole arm disappears. . . . You then watch as the rest of your body disappears. . . . Only your head is floating in space, and then it, too, disappears. . . . Now your whole body has disappeared. . . .

But where your body used to be is now a beautiful glowing blue-white light. . . . And you still look like you. . . . You still have feet and legs and arms and hands and everything. . . . Only this time, you are made of beautifully glowing light, and all you can feel is love. . . . And now, because you are made of light, you can go anywhere you want to go, as fast as you like to, and stay as long as you want to stay. . . . *Sweet Dreams!*

The Values Goals

All known behavior is the result of enhancements or deprivations of the eight basic needs and wants, or values goals described below.

1.   *Affection* is getting and giving friendship and love, caring about and being concerned for others, and having others care and be concerned about you.

2.   *Enlightenment* or knowing is understanding the meaning of things; being able to apply that knowledge to meet your goals, being able to learn new things, and affording others the opportunity to learn new things.

3.   *Respect* is looking up to or admiring people and having them do the same toward you and others.

4.   *Responsibility* is knowing as well as doing what is correct for yourself and others; being trustworthy, honest, fair; and establishing and living by rules that protect the rights, freedom, and the opportunities and property of all created beings.

5.   *Power* is controlling your own behavior and having the ability to make your own choices; being able to influence others to do what you want them to do; and being able to share in decisions made by others that affect you.

6.   *Skill* is learning how to do things well, doing them well, feeling that you can do them well.

7.   *Wealth* is having the opportunity to get the goods and services that you need.

8.   *Well-Being* is feeling healthy, happy, and generally well.